Never Pet a Penguin

By Mariah Clark Skewes
Illustrated by Phoebe Cho

Li'l hedgehog™ PUBLISHING

Dedicated to

Ian, Trevor, & Sammy

Who would NEVER pet a penguin.....

.....or maybe, just maybe, they would!

ISBN 979-8-9881114-8-1

"NEVER PET A PENGUIN!" Nana said.

I told her I wouldn't and I knew that I shouldn't.......
but then I thought, if I'm very, VERY, VERY careful,
maybe I could do it just once and Nana wouldn't really mind.

And I really, REALLY, REALLY
wanted to pet a penguin!

So, I headed down the steps to find a penguin to pet.

I went into the garden –

and into the fields nearby –

and even into the woods.

I searched everywhere I thought a penguin might hide.
I found mice, skunks, hawks, and peacocks, and even
a couple of hedgehogs and fish!

But I didn't find any penguins!

I explored our town. I found dogs, cats, and turtles and even some chickens, two sheep and a goat. But I didn't find any penguins.

I visited the animal shelter with Nana.
I found kittens, puppies, and rabbits and
even some guinea pigs and two parakeets.
But I still didn't find any penguins.

I went to the zoo with my school.
I found leopards, elephants, ostriches, giraffes,
and zebras, and even some alligators, pythons, and tarantulas.
But I still didn't find any penguins.
Where were all the penguins?

When we returned to school, I asked our librarian for help. She said that most penguins live near the South Pole.

That's 8,762 miles away from my house and there's not even a walking route to get there!

She said penguins also live in South Africa – 10,409 miles away! And in New Zealand - only 7,141 miles. Galapagos Islands penguins are the closest – just 3,324 miles. But that's in the middle of the ocean and way too far to swim.

Back at home, I decided I needed a boat to reach the penguins.
I found some old boards and a rope,
a wooden broom handle and a tarp.
I tied the boards together and made a mast and a sail.
But when I put my boat in the pond, it didn't even float!

Maybe a hot air balloon would work!

I found some leftover birthday balloons and blew them up.

I tied them onto a wicker laundry basket with some string and waited for the wind. But we didn't even get off the ground.

How about flying to the penguins? I needed wings.
I collected hawk feathers and peacock feathers.

I glued them together and tied them onto my arms.
I flapped and flapped, but I didn't fly.
Not even one little bit!

That night, I felt pretty sad.
If I couldn't get to the penguins,
how was I ever going to be able to pet one?

But the next morning Nana surprised me.
"Guess what, Maddy?
We're going to the Marine Park this weekend to see The Cold Zone Exhibit. There are polar bear families in one area and penguin colonies in another."

Penguins at the Marine Park?!?! COOLY-OH, I thought.
Maybe I'll be able to pet one after all!

When we got to the Marine Park, I couldn't believe it.
There were penguins everywhere!

"Would you like to pet a penguin?" the penguin keeper asked.
Would I ever! Nana smiled.

"Do you think we could bring a penguin home with us?" I asked.

"Your house would have to be a cold zone filled with ice and glaciers for a real penguin to be happy there," the penguin keeper replied. "But how about taking this little one home instead?"

That night, Nana tucked me into bed and kissed me goodnight.
"I'm glad you got to pet your penguin after all,"
she said as she turned out the light.

"Me, too," I smiled.
Hmmm......I thought......
ideas drifting through my mind as I fell asleep.....
our house a cold zone....
filled with snow and ice cubes....
maybe, just maybe.......

ABOUT THE AUTHOR:

Mariah Clark Skewes, known in her real life as Mary Boyle, knows from experience that children have individual personalities that can be shaped, but not changed – her own four adult children are unique and talented, each following their own dreams. Mariah/Mary's degrees in Psychology and Special Education have guided her work with children for many years as both a teacher and school administrator, specializing in connecting with those kiddos who sometimes have presented the greatest challenges – yet yielded the greatest rewards. She and her husband live on a vineyard in the Sierra Nevada foothills of Northern California where they grow wine grapes and raise honeybees and Southdown Babydoll Sheep. When not writing, she enjoys volunteering as a CASA with children in the foster care system, competing in world marathons and travelling.

ABOUT THE ILLUSTRATOR:

Phoebe Cho is a talented illustrator who loves travel, surfing, biking, and collaborating on children's picture books. Originally from South Korea, Phoebe has lived in Portugal and now calls the United Kingdom home. Her artistic specialty is the drawing of children and adults, with fine attention to facial expressions. She has a unique talent for capturing the emotions of a story's characters and bringing them to life for the reader. Phoebe graduated from the University of Brighton, with a Bachelor of Arts Degree in Illustration and is now a freelance illustrator for books, advertisements, and educational materials. She describes her style as organic and warm, yet modern and quirky through her use of texture, shape and color.

SUPPORT FOR CHILDREN AND FAMILIES:

For information on brain research and learning differences including ADHD, Schizophrenia, and Autism, visit UC Davis Mind Institute at www.health.ucdavis.edu/mindinstitute

For information on volunteering with children in Foster Care in your area, visit CASA/GAL at www.nationalcasagal.org

For information on adopting waiting children, visit AdoptUSKids.org

More Books by Mariah Clark Skewes

(Mary Boyle)

Published or Coming Soon!

Picture Books

The NEVER Series & Activity Books:
Never Hug a Hedgehog;
Never Kiss a Fish;
Never Mimic a Woolly Mammoth
Quirky Grandma Jean
SMUDGE!
O is for Pig
King Betterist
Jordan
Best Friends

For Middle Grades

Molly's World—A collection of Short Stories

For Young Adults

Maddie's in the Middle
(An inpiring novel of overcoming circumstances)

And for Adults

The ABC's of Hope & Healing
(A Gift Book)

Books available on amazon.com and barnesandnoble.com
and in local bookstores by request

Milton Keynes UK
Ingram Content Group UK Ltd.
UKHW051429050424
440471UK00011B/48

9 798988 111481